BIG PUZZLES
FOR
Little Hands

Ages 3-8

People Who Obeyed God

Carla Williams

For information regarding the CPSIA on this printed material call:
203-595-3636 and provide reference # LANC-315751

rainbowpublishers®

www.RainbowPublishers.com

Dedication

To my sons, Joshua and Josiah, whose love and obedience toward God give me hope through puzzling times.

BIG PUZZLES FOR LITTLE HANDS: PEOPLE WHO OBEYED GOD
©2011 by Rainbow Publishers, eighth printing
ISBN 10: 1-885358-48-2
ISBN 13: 978-1-885358-48-6
Rainbow reorder #RB36831
RELIGION / Christian Ministry / Children

Rainbow Publishers
P.O. Box 261129
San Diego, CA 92196
www.RainbowPublishers.com

Interior Illustrator: Chuck Galey
Cover Illustrator: Court Patton

Scriptures are from the Holy Bible: *New International Version* (North American Edition), copyright ©1973, 1978, 1984 by the International Bible Society. Used by permission of Zondervan Bible Publishers.

Permission is granted to the buyer of this book to photocopy student materials for use with Sunday school or Bible teaching classes.

Printed in the United States of America

Table *of* Contents

Introduction

Young children are very inquisitive and love to learn new things — the most important of which are Bible truths. Because developmental growth in your small students involves eye-hand coordination and perceptual skills, puzzles and pencil activities are excellent tools for teaching spiritual concepts to little ones.

The activities in *Big Puzzles for Little Hands* help children strengthen their language, counting, comparison and thinking skills. Even the youngest child, still uncoordinated with pencil or crayon, can use his or her fingers to point to pictures or follow mazes. With the variety of topics — over 75 different lessons! — you are sure to find puzzles related to your class curriculum. Or, consider using the puzzle sheets as complete lessons (suggested Bible story discussion points are included with each puzzle). Either way, be sure to send the puzzle sheet home with your students. They will be proud to show their parents their completed puzzles and the Scripture and story on the sheets will cue parents to the day's lesson points.

Before you begin, here are a few hints to make the most of *Big Puzzles for Little Hands*:

- Consult the scripture index on page 7 to quickly match a puzzle with your curriculum.
- Consider duplicating two related sheets back-to-back for class use and home extension.
- Read the instructions for the activity to the children. You will also need to read aloud any wording within the worksheet.
- Review the memory verse with the children as they work on the puzzles. Even though preschoolers cannot read, they are able to learn Scripture through repetition.
- The puzzles vary in difficulty to meet the needs of your class. More advanced children will find the number and letter puzzles enjoyable, while younger students will enjoy the coloring-based activities.
- Review activities are included at the end of each section.
- In addition to Sunday school, *Big Puzzles for Little Hands* are a great resource for children's church, pew activities and family devotionals.
- Answers to the puzzles are on pages 95 and 96.

Scripture Index

Old Testament

The Old Testament is rich with examples of people who struggled with obeying God. There are those like Moses who began as a reluctant leader but by obeying God became a great man for Him. There is Jonah, a man chosen by God who unsuccessfully tried to escape His instruction. And then there is Job, one who faced great difficulties but obeyed God through it all. The following lessons and puzzles will help your students see that obeying God and those in authority is the right thing to do.

Noah Obeys God

Memory Verse

Noah did everything just as God commanded him.
~Genesis 6:22

Teacher Talk

Use the Noah Match to review the story of Noah. Ask, **What did God tell Noah to build?** Noah obeyed God. **How many of each animal did God tell Noah to take on the boat? Can you find the turtles that are like the first ones? What kind of bird did Noah send out of the boat? What did God put in the sky? Can you obey God like Noah did?**

Noah Match

Look at the pictures in each row. Color the pictures in each row that look the same as the first picture in that row.

Noah Leads the Animals

Memory Verse

Pairs of all creatures came to Noah.
~Genesis 7:15

Teacher Talk

God must have spoken to the animals and told them to follow Noah into the ark. Discuss with your children that the animals had to obey God, too. Say, **The animals obeyed God and Noah and were saved from the Flood.**

▶ The Animals Obeyed God

Draw a line to each animal pair's shadow.

The Dove Returns to the Ark

Memory Verse

The dove returned to him.
~Genesis 8:11

Teacher Talk

Lead the children in a discussion of how Noah and his family might have felt while in the ark. Use the maze to discuss what Noah could have been thinking while waiting for the dove to return. Say, Noah obeyed God and stayed in the ark until God said it was time to come out. We should obey God, too, and live as He says.

Help the Dove Return to the Ark

Follow the maze with your finger or a pencil.

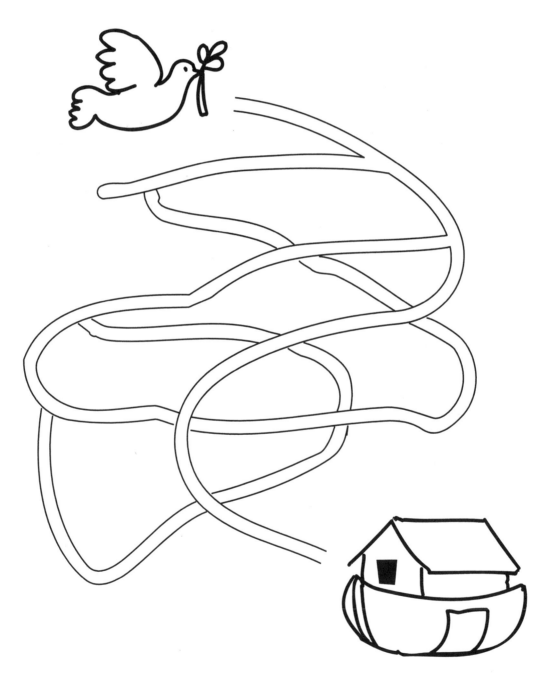

Rainbow of Promise

Memory Verse

Praise the Lord, you who obey his word.
~Psalm 103:20

Teacher Talk

Say, Noah obeyed God. God took care of Noah and his family and all of the animals. Obeying God made Noah happy. He built an altar to God. He thanked God and praised Him. God sent a beautiful rainbow. The rainbow was God's promise never to flood the earth again. God keeps His promises to us.

See God's Promise

Connect the dots in each row with a different color of crayon.

13

Abraham Moves to Canaan

Memory Verse

By faith Abraham obeyed and went.
~Hebrews 11:8

Teacher Talk

Ask, Have you ever moved to a new home? Allow the children to respond. Ask, **How did you feel?** Abraham left his home and traveled far away. **God told him where to go. Abraham obeyed God.** Use the activity to discuss the different places Abraham could have gone. Ask, What kinds of things might have happened at the other places? Younger children may simply color the picture while older ones can also complete the word puzzle.

Where Did God Send Abraham?

Cross out the lower-case letters. The letters that remain tell where Abraham went. Then color the picture.

wCrtAqNpzAgiAkN

As Numerous as the Stars

Memory Verse

You will be the father of many nations.
~Genesis 17:4

Teacher Talk

Ask, How many brothers and sisters do you have? Do you have cousins? God told Abraham that He would make him the father of many nations. This meant that he would have lots and lots of children and grandchildren. And then they would have children and there would be many aunts, uncles and cousins. In fact, God said that Abraham would have as many children as there are stars in the sky. Can you count the stars in the sky? You can count the stars on this sheet but you cannot count the stars in the sky. Abraham became the father of a great nation.

·············► The Father of Many Nations

Find the stars and color them. How many stars can you count?

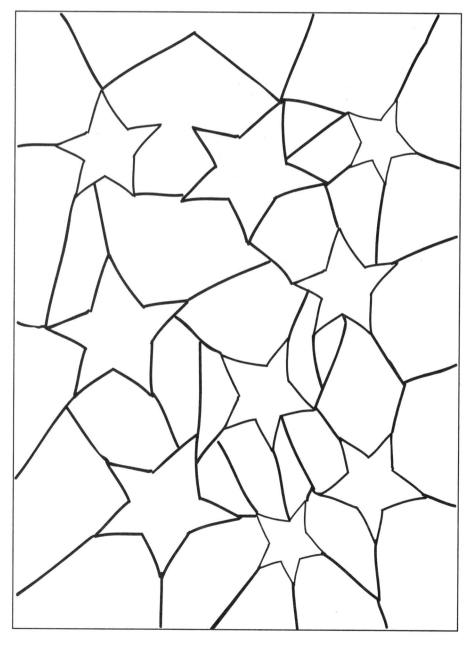

The Promised Son

Memory Verse

The Lord is faithful to all his promises.
~Psalm 145:13

Teacher Talk

Say, Abraham did not have any children for a long time, even though God had promised him he would. His wife, Sarah, was really old and Abraham was really old. It looked like God would not keep His promise to Abraham. But Abraham kept obeying and trusting God. Soon Abraham and Sarah had a baby boy.

A Special Blessing

Look at the pictures below. Which special blessing did God give Abraham and Sarah? Draw it in their arms.

16

True Obedience

Memory Verse

Obey the Lord your God.
~Jeremiah 26:13

Teacher Talk

Say, God wanted to see how much Abraham loved Him and would obey Him. God told Abraham to take his son, Isaac, to a mountain top. God told Abraham to sacrifice, or kill, his son. Abraham obeyed God. Just as Abraham was ready to kill Isaac, the angel of the Lord stopped him. Now God knew that Abraham loved Him and would obey Him always. God gave Abraham a ram to sacrifice in place of his son. We should show God we love Him by obeying.

Abraham Obeyed God

Color the picture, then cut it into four pieces along the heavy, black lines. Mix up the pieces and put the picture back together!

17

An Obedient Son

Memory Verse
Children, obey your parents.
~Ephesians 6:1

Teacher Talk
Say, Jacob had twelve sons. Joseph was Jacob's favorite son. Joseph worked hard for his father. He tended the sheep and took food to his older brothers working in the fields. Joseph was a good boy and obeyed his father, so his father gave him a special coat. If you obey God, His special gift to you will be to live with Him forever in heaven.

Which Is Not Complete?
One picture in each of the rows below is only half-finished. Select those that are not complete and fill in the missing parts so they match the others.

18

Joseph Trusted God

Memory Verse
Trust in the Lord.
~Proverbs 3:5

Teacher Talk
Say, Joseph loved God. Joseph was a good boy and his father loved him very much. But Joseph's brothers did not like him. One day they sold him into slavery. Joseph trusted God to take care of him, even in bad times. We can always trust God to take care of us.

▶ God Cares for Joseph
Color the picture. Connect the dots in each letter to read the word.

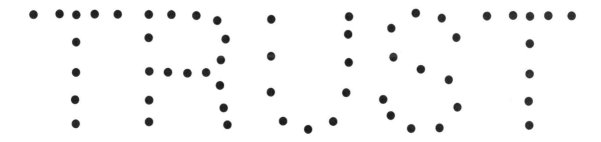

A Story to Tell

Memory Verse
The Lord was with Joseph.
~Genesis 39:23

Teacher Talk
Use the pictures to tell the events of Joseph's life in Egypt. Have younger children point to the pictures instead of writing numbers. Say, **Joseph's master became angry with him and threw him into prison. While Joseph was in prison, the king of Egypt had two dreams. Joseph told the king what the dreams meant. The king was pleased. He made Joseph an important man. Joseph was reunited with his family. God helped Joseph to turn a bad time into a good one.**

Joseph in Egypt
These pictures of Joseph are all mixed up. Can you number them in the correct order? The first one is done for you.

Joseph Forgives His Brothers

Memory Verse

Be kind and compassionate to one another, forgiving each other.
~Ephesians 4:32

Teacher Talk

Say, Joseph had many struggles. His brothers treated him very badly. Yet Joseph obeyed God and forgave his brothers. Do you forgive your brothers and sisters when they do something wrong to you?

Find Joseph's Brothers

Hidden in this picture are 11 faces. Can you find and color them?

21

Moses and the Burning Bush

Memory Verse
We must obey God.
~Acts 5:29

Teacher Talk
Say, One day Moses saw a bush. The bush was burning. God talked to Moses from the bush. God told Moses, "Go to Egypt." Moses was afraid to go there. But he knew God would help him. Moses obeyed God and went to Egypt. God will always help us to do what He asks.

⋯⋯► The Burning Bush
Color all of the diamonds red and the triangles orange, then color the rest of the picture.

Ten Warnings

Memory Verse

All rulers will worship and obey him.
~Daniel 7:27

Teacher Talk

Say, Moses told the king of Egypt, "Let my people go!" The king was angry and said, "No! They will stay my slaves!" Then God sent ten warnings to the king. Bad things began to happen. The king kept telling Moses, "No!" So God sent His last warning. The king's oldest son died. Now the king of Egypt knew that God was real. He let Moses and the people leave. God doesn't like it when we disobey Him, but He takes care of those who do obey Him.

·············▶ God Warned Pharoah

Count the creatures, then color the picture.

How many ?   How many ?   How many ?

Moses Crosses the Red Sea

Memory Verse

The people put their trust in him.
~Exodus 14:31

Teacher Talk

Guide the children in a discussion about Moses leading the people out of Egypt. Say, **The king of Egypt changed his mind. He chased Moses and his people. When the people saw a huge sea (called the Red Sea) in front of them they got scared. But Moses told the people not to be afraid. "God will help us!" he said. And God did! He parted the sea! The people crossed onto dry land, then God closed the sea so the soldiers could not cross. God took care of Moses and His people, and He takes care of us.**

Crossing the Red Sea

Help Moses lead the Israelites across the Red Sea. Follow the path with a pencil or crayon.

24

Ten Rules to Obey

Memory Verse
I will obey your word.
~Psalm 119:17

Teacher Talk
Say, God had some very special rules He wanted the people to obey. God told Moses to go high on a mountain. There God wrote ten rules on stone called the Ten Commandments. He gave the stones to Moses. Moses told the people the rules. Some of the people obeyed the rules. Do you want to obey God's rules? Obeying God's rules makes us happy.

God's Rules
Connect the dots to see where God wrote His rules.

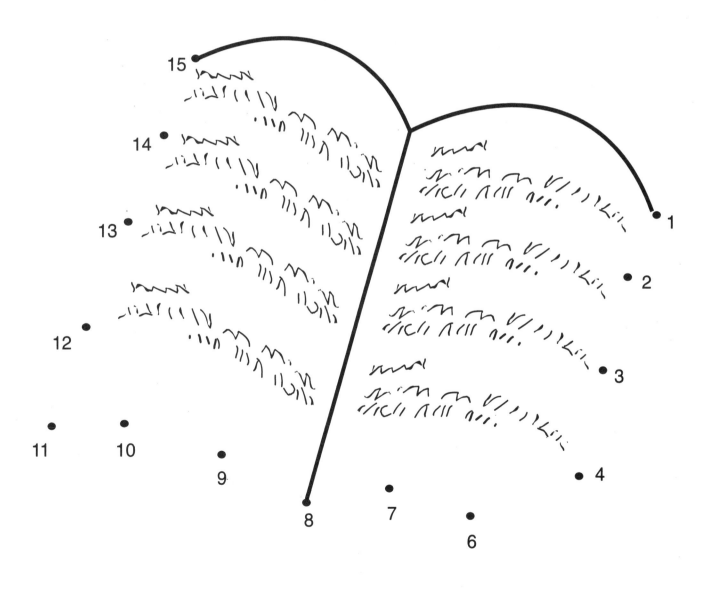

25

God Tells His People to Obey Him

Memory Verse

Keep the commands of the Lord your God.
~Deuteronomy 4:2

Teacher Talk

Say, After God brought the Israelites out of Egypt they needed rules to govern their lives. We all need rules to live by, otherwise there is confusion and disorder. So God gave His people rules that would help them love and care for each other and worship Him. Discuss with your children why rules are good. Read each rule at left and ask them to select the picture that goes with that rule.

Obeying God's Rules

Draw a line from the rule on the left to the picture that matches it on the right.

Obey Your Mother and Father.

Make God's Day Special!

Do Not Steal.

God Gives His People Rules

Memory Verse
These commandments that I give you today are to be upon your hearts.
~Deuteronomy 6:6

Teacher Talk
Say, God wrote His rules on tablets of stone, but He wanted the people to keep the rules in their hearts. Talk with your children about how we can keep God's laws in our hearts by good behavior and prayer.

Where Are God's Rules?
Write the first letter of each object to finish this sentence starting with the hat.

God's rules are on your _____ .

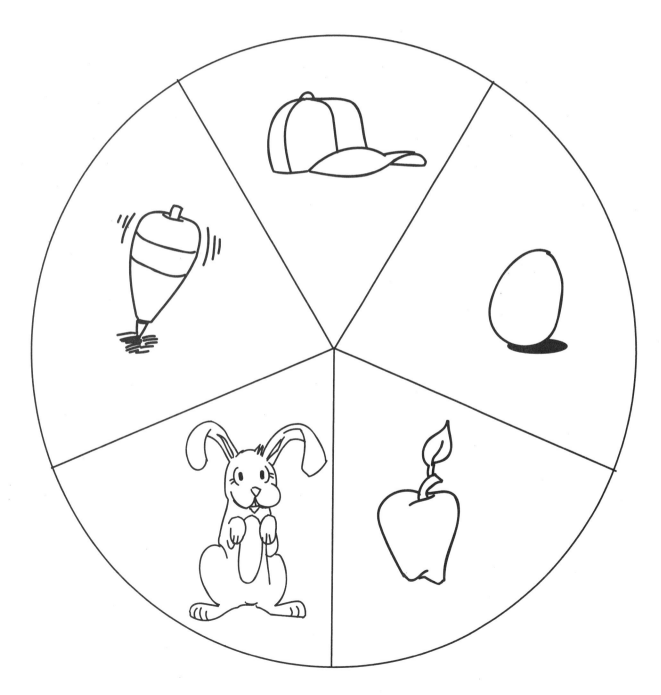

God's People Disobey Him

Memory Verse

I brought you up out of Egypt yet you have disobeyed me.
~Judges 2:1-2

Teacher Talk

Here is a story that teaches that disobedience has consequences. Say, **The people of Israel forgot all the things God had done for them and began worshiping idols. As a result, God disciplined them by allowing the nations around Israel to defeat them.** Use this lesson to discuss what happens when we disobey.

Which Child Is Obedient?

Circle the obedient children. Make an X on the disobedient ones.

God's Rules are Good

Memory Verse
Keep my commands and follow them. I am the Lord.
~Leviticus 22:31

Teacher Talk
Discuss with your children that God's rules are for our good and protection. Ask, **Which rules are easy to obey? Which ones are harder to obey?**

Keeping the Rules
Each of these children needs something to obey God's rules. Draw a line to the objects they need.

God Calls Gideon

Memory Verse
The Lord answered, "I will be with you."
~Judges 6:16

Teacher Talk
Say, Gideon was a young man who was very fearful. Yet he overcame his fears and learned to obey everything the Lord asked of him. Use this puzzle to help you tell the story of Gideon's encounter with the angel of the Lord.

The Lord Accepts Gideon's Offering
Connect the broken lines to see the sign the angel gave Gideon. Color the picture.

Gideon Defeats His Enemies

Memory Verse
A sword for the Lord and for Gideon!
~Judges 7:20

Teacher Talk
Say, **The Lord spoke to Gideon in a dream. God promised to help Gideon defeat the Midianites.** Tell your children the story from the book of Judges about the wonderful way that Gideon defeated his enemies.

············► **A Sword for the Lord**

Hidden in this picture are 3 , 6 and 10 . Can you find them?

Obey and Don't Be Afraid

Memory Verse
Be strong and courageous.
~Joshua 1:6

Teacher Talk
Say, Moses led the people to a new land. But God wanted Moses to join Him in heaven. So God told Joshua to lead the people into the new land. Joshua was very young. God told him, "Don't be afraid. I will help you lead the people." Joshua obeyed God and led the people in the new land. God can help us to do things that we think we cannot do on our own.

Joshua Led the Israelites
Count the shapes and write the number of each in the blanks.

How many □'s? _____

How many △'s? _____

How many ○'s? _____

Rahab Obeys the True God

Memory Verse
Have no other gods before me.
~Deuteronomy 5:7

Teacher Talk
Say, Joshua led the people to the new land. They came to a city called Jericho. The people in Jericho did not worship God. They worshiped gods of stone and wood. A woman named Rahab lived in Jericho. Rahab decided to obey God and help Joshua. We should obey God and help others, too.

Rahab Helped the Joshua's Men
Color the pictures, then circle the soldier in the bottom picture who is marching DOWN the hill.

33

Jericho Falls

Memory Verse
We will serve the Lord our God and obey him.
~Joshua 24:24

Teacher Talk
Say, God told Joshua to march around Jericho everyday. On the seventh day God said, "Tell the people to march around the city seven times. On the seventh time, blow the horns and shout loudly! The walls will fall down." Joshua and the people obeyed. The walls of Jericho came falling down. We can do incredible things if we obey God's commands!

▶ Matching Marchers
God told the people to march around Jericho. In each row, color the people who are marching the same way.

34

A Faithful Friend

Memory Verse

Where you go I will go.
~Ruth 1:16

Teacher Talk

Say, Naomi's husband and sons died. Naomi was all alone. But one of Naomi's sons had a lovely wife named Ruth. Ruth said she would always stay with Naomi. Naomi taught Ruth about God. Ruth learned to love and obey Naomi's God—the same God we worship today. We can share about our God with family and friends, too.

What's the Difference?

Ruth and Naomi were best friends. How many things can you find in the bottom picture that are different from the top one?

God Blesses Ruth's Obedience

Memory Verse

He who obeys instructions guards his life.
Proverbs 19:16

Teacher Talk

Say, Naomi and Ruth were hungry. Naomi instructed Ruth to go to Boaz's fields and glean from his harvest. Ruth obeyed Naomi. Boaz looked favorably on Ruth because she was kind and obedient to Naomi. He allowed her to have as much grain as she needed. God takes care of those who obey Him.

Ruth Gathers Grain

Color each space that contains a letter. What do you see?

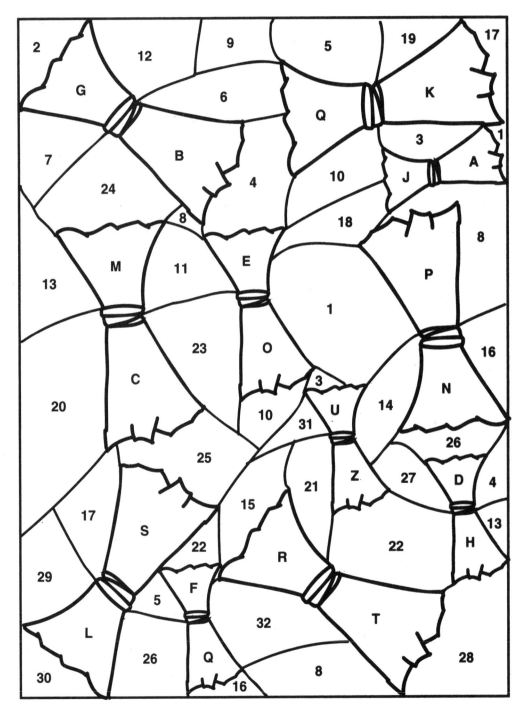

A Mother Keeps Her Promise

Memory Verse
Everyone has heard about your obedience, so I am full of joy
~Romans 16:19

Teacher Talk
Say, Hannah wanted a baby. Hannah promised that she would take her child to God's house, the tabernacle. God gave Hannah a special son. Hannah named him Samuel. When Samuel was old enough, Hannah kept her promise. She took him to the tabernacle. God rewards those who keep their promises to Him.

Find the Tabernacle
Help Hannah and Samuel get to the tabernacle by following the path.

Disobedient Sons

Memory Verse

They were disobedient and rebelled against [God].
~Nehemiah 9:26

Teacher Talk

Say, Samuel grew up in the tabernacle. He was a good boy. Samuel obeyed Eli, the priest. Eli had two sons of his own but they did not obey their father. Eli's sons were disobedient. We should show God's love and always be obedient.

⋯⋯⋯▶ Good Behavior

Draw a line to the pictures that show the opposite of Samuel's good actions.

Samuel Obeys God's Call

Memory Verse

Listen to what I say to you.
~Ezekiel 2:8

Teacher Talk

Say, Samuel loved God. Samuel also loved God's house. One night God talked to Samuel. God told Samuel some things He planned to do. Samuel listened and obeyed God. We should listen to God, too.

Samuel Obeyed God

Hidden in this picture are an oil lamp, a water pitcher, a lamb, a scroll and a patched robe. Can you find them?

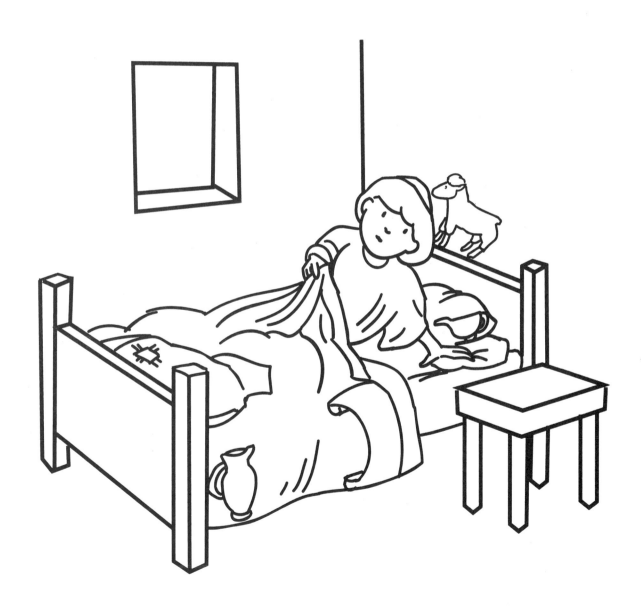

Samuel Finds Israel a King

Memory Verse

The Lord answered, "Listen to them and give them a king."
~1 Samuel 8:22

Teacher Talk

Say, Obeying just God wasn't enough for the Israelites. The people wanted a king to obey. God told Samuel to find the people a king. Samuel warned the people that a king would be hard to obey. Do you think it would be hard to obey a king?

Israel Crowns a King

How many crowns can you find in this picture? Color them.

God Calls David

Memory Verse

The Lord looks at the heart.
~1 Samuel 16:7

Teacher Talk

Say, David watched his father's sheep. He took very good care of them. When the people needed a new king, God picked David. David made a good king because he was a good shepherd who took care of his flock. God likes it when we work hard and follow Him.

God Calls a Shepherd Boy

Color the spaces with A white. Color the spaces with B green. Color the spaces with C blue. Color the spaces with D brown. Color the spaces with E black.

Obedience Kills a Giant

Memory Verse
Your servant will go and fight [Goliath].
~1 Samuel 17:32

Teacher Talk
Say, When David was a little boy, he wanted to fight Goliath, a giant. The grown-up soldiers laughed at him. So did the king. "How could a small boy fight a giant?" they asked. "God will help me!" said David. And He did! Use the pictures below to help you tell the story. Discuss how the story would change if the differences between the two pictures were true.

▶ David Fights the Giant
Find seven things in the bottom picture that are different from the top one.

Good Friends

Memory Verse

Submit to one another.
~Ephesians 5:21

Teacher Talk

Say, **Jonathan knew that David obeyed and trusted God. He knew that God helped David kill Goliath. Jonathan liked that David followed God so he and David became best friends. He was able to help David and David helped him, too.** Discuss with the children that submitting means that we are nice to our friends and family. Suggest some situations, such as choosing a game, when a friend could submit to another friend.

Being a Friend

What do good friends do? Write the first letter of each picture in the space below it.

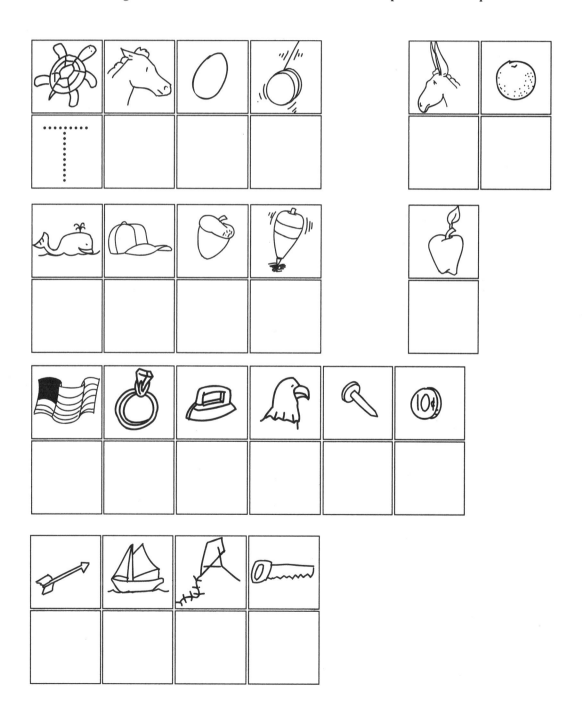

A Special Gift

Bible Story:
1 Kings 3:5-15

Memory Verse

If any of you lacks wisdom, he should ask God.
~James 1:5

Teacher Talk

Say, Solomon had a big job as king. He had a lot of choices to make. God knew that Solomon wanted to be a good king. So one day, God asked Solomon if he could have anything in the whole world what would it be. What do you think Solomon asked for? He asked for wisdom to make good choices. God was very pleased with Solomon. He gave him a special gift of wisdom. God gives each of us special gifts.

Wise Choices

Some of the children in the picture below are making wise choices and some of them are not. Color the children that have the gift of wisdom.

Building God's House

Memory Verse

Let us go to the house of the Lord.
~Psalm 122:1

Teacher Talk

Say, King Solomon loved God. He wanted to show God how much he loved Him. So King Solomon decided to build a special house for God where the people could talk to Him. Solomon built a beautiful house for God. Then Solomon told all of the people, "Come worship at God's house." God loves when we come to church and worship Him.

The Way to the Temple

First help the workers find God's house. Then help Solomon and the people find their way to worship there.

Bad Friends

Memory Verse

Bad company corrupts good character.
~1 Corinthians 15:33

Teacher Talk

Say, Solomon didn't always make wise choices. As his kingdom grew, Solomon gained many friends. Some of these friends worshiped idols and not God. Solomon allowed these friends to worship idols in his land. Soon all the people forgot God and began worshiping idols. Solomon allowed idols and his friends to come between him and God. We should not allow anything to come between us and following God.

⋯⋯⋯⋯➤ In the Way

Circle what is BETWEEN Solomon and the temple in each picture.

The True God

Memory Verse

The Lord — he is God!
~1 Kings 18:39

Teacher Talk

Say, Some foolish people believed that Baal was the true God. But Elijah knew differently. One day he decided to prove the true God. So he built an altar and put meat on it. He told the foolish people to ask Baal to send fire down on the altar. Nothing happened. Elijah poured water on the altar. He prayed and asked God to send fire. God sent fire from heaven on the altar. Our God is stronger than any fake idol that people create.

➤ An Altared Drawing

Can you draw an altar? Trace over the dots to fill in the boxes in the grid, then look at the example and draw what is missing in the empty boxes.

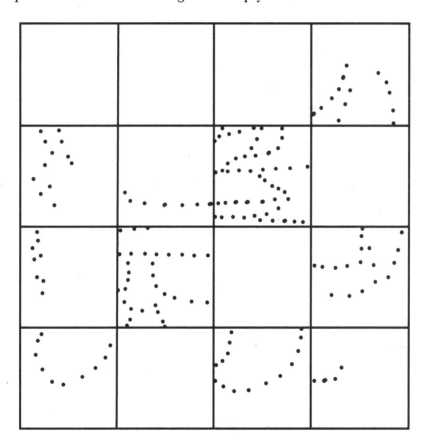

God Takes Care of Elijah

Bible Story:
1 Kings 17:1-5

Memory Verse

He cares for those who trust in Him.
~Nahum 1:7

Teacher Talk

Say, A wicked king ruled Israel. He encouraged the people to worship idols. God told Elijah to go deep into the woods because He was going to punish Israel. For many years there would be no rain in the land. Elijah trusted and obeyed God. He had no food to eat, but God sent Elijah food in a special way.

God Feeds Elijah

Color BLACK all the spaces with dots.
Color YELLOW the spaces with stars.
Color the empty spaces light blue.
How did God feed Elijah?

Elisha Follows Elijah

Memory Verse

I will keep your law and obey it with all my heart.
Psalm 119:34

Teacher Talk

Say, The prophet Elijah had a follower named Elisha. Elisha wanted to learn all about following God. He asked Elijah to give him a double portion of his spirit. Elisha wanted to understand all he could about God's power so he could teach the people to obey.

⋯⋯⋯➤ What's Different?

How many things in the top picture are different from the one below it?

Elisha Makes Bad Water Clean

Memory Verse
Be careful to obey.
~Deuteronomy 6:3

Teacher Talk
Say, God performed many miracles through His prophets. Elisha was careful to obey God's commands and to teach others to do the same. As a result, God could show His power through Elisha. Read the story of Elisha healing the bad water to your children.

● ● ● ● ● ● ● ● ● ► God Helped Elisha
How did Elisha make the water clean? Write down the names in the pictures and add or subtract the letters to find out.

HELP - LP ___ ___

3 - E + W ___ ___ ___ ___ ___

 - W + L T ___ ___ ___ ___ ___

- T ___ ___

3 - R E ___ ___ ___

W + - C + ER ___ ___ ___ ___ ___

50

Hezekiah Does What Is Right

Memory Verse

[Hezekiah] did what was right in the eyes of the Lord.
~2 Chronicles 29:2

Teacher Talk

Say, **The Israelites had turned their backs on God and the temple was in shambles. When Hezekiah became king, he repaired the temple and purified the priests.** Discuss with your children why the Bible says that Hezekiah "did what was right in the eyes of the Lord." Ask, **What things can you do that might be "right" in God's eyes?**

Hezekiah Repaired the Temple

Cut out the puzzle pieces and put them together correctly.

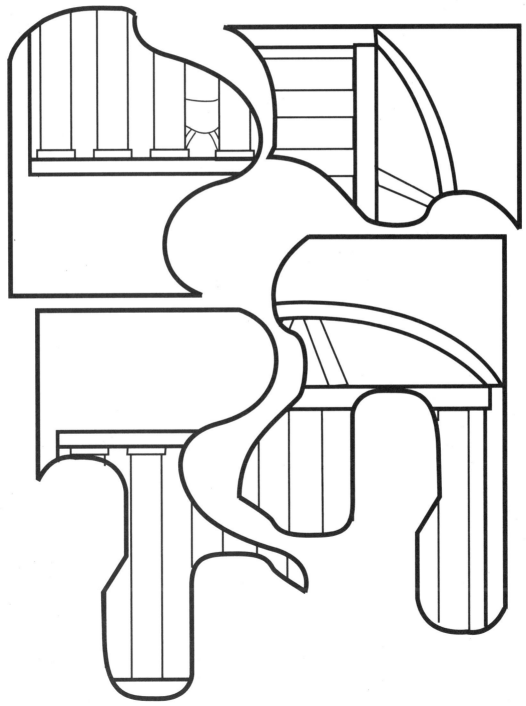

Hezekiah Celebrates the Passover

Memory Verse

There was great joy in Jerusalem.
~2 Chronicles 30:26

Teacher Talk

Say, After Hezekiah purified the temple, he decided it was time for Israel to celebrate the Passover. Hezekiah told the people that they must remember all that the Lord had done for them. For seven days the people celebrated with instruments of praise and offerings to the Lord. There had not been so much joy in Jerusalem since the time of King Solomon. God heard the prayers of the people and turned His anger from them.

Memory Game

Study this page for a minute. Then cover the page. See how many things you can remember and tell them to a partner. Then have your partner take a turn.

Hezekiah Repents of His Pride

Memory Verse

Hezekiah repented of the pride of his heart.
~2 Chronicles 32:26

Teacher Talk

Say, Hezekiah did many great things to restore Israel. However, Hezekiah soon became prideful and forgot the kindness the Lord had shown him. God was angry with Hezekiah's disobedience. But then the king repented of his pride. God was happy that Hezekiah obeyed Him again.

Crossword Puzzle

In the squares going down write the name of the picture above. Then read across to fill in the blank below.

Hezekiah's _____ caused him to disobey God.

Nehemiah Looks at the Walls of Jerusalem

Bible Story:
Nehemiah 2:11-16

Memory Verse

We have not obeyed the commands, decrees and laws.
~Nehemiah 1:7

Teacher Talk

Say, Nehemiah was very sad when he heard that the walls of Jerusalem were torn down. He confessed the disobedience of the people. When he went to Jerusalem, he rode on a horse around the city to see how much damage had occurred.

A Sad Ride

Nehemiah has lost his horse. Can you help him find it? Color it in when you do.

Repairing the Walls

Memory Verse

Let us rebuild the wall.
~Nehemiah 2:17

Teacher Talk

Say, Jerusalem was a beautiful city. But the Babylonian soldiers tore it down. The walls were in terrible condition for years. Nehemiah said to the king, "Let me go and repair the walls of Jerusalem." The king liked Nehemiah and agreed. Nehemiah worked hard to obey God and rebuild the city. God was pleased. God expects us to work hard to obey Him.

Good as New

Draw a line from each stone to where it fits in the wall.

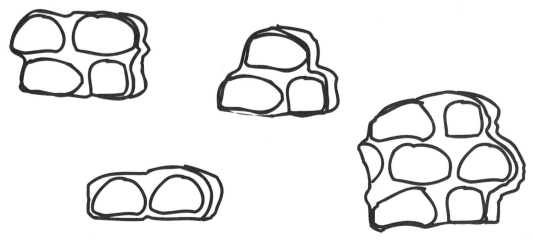

A Beautiful Queen Obeys

Memory Verse
I have obeyed my Father's commands.
~John 15:10

Teacher Talk
Say, The king needed a new queen. He picked Esther. Esther was beautiful. The king gave her beautiful clothes and jewelry. She was a successful queen because she allowed God to use her. God can use each of us if we give Him control of our lives.

⋯⋯⋯▶ Help Esther
Esther is getting ready to see the king. Draw a line from Esther to the clothes she might have worn to visit the king.

56

Esther Obeys
Mordecai's Instruction

Memory Verse

Whoever gives heed to instruction prospers.
~Proverbs 16:20

Teacher Talk

Say, Esther was really frightened when she heard what her Uncle Mordecai wanted her to say to the king. No one was allowed to go before the king unless invited. Esther was afraid that the king might have her put to death. But for the sake of her people, she decided to do everything her Uncle Mordecai told her and talked to the king. The king listened to her.

Can You Find Esther?

There are many people waiting to see the king. Look for Queen Esther and circle her, then color the picture.

57

Job Obeys No Matter What

Memory Verse
In all this, Job did not sin.
~Job 1:22

Teacher Talk
Say, Job obeyed God even when bad things happened. Lots of bad things happened to Job, but Job still trusted God. God took care of Job because he obeyed Him. God is with us even when bad things happen. Use the story puzzles to tell Job's story.

▶ Making Sense of Job
These pictures tell about Job. But they are all mixed up. Can you number them in the correct order? The first one is done for you.

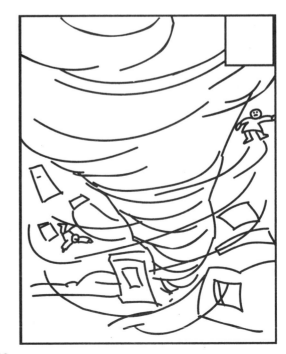

Job's Friends Try to Make Him Disobey

Bible Story:
Job 2-37

Memory Verse
How long will you torment me and crush me with words?
~Job 19:2

Teacher Talk
Say, Job's wife and three friends tried to get him to curse God and give up. But Job refused to disobey God. Discuss with your children about times when friends try to get them to disobey God. Ask, What could you say if a friend tried to make you disobey God?

⤑ Which Way?
Help Job find the altar.

59

The King's Food

Memory Verse

Whatever you do, do it all for the glory of God.
~1 Corinthians 10:31

Teacher Talk

Say, Daniel and his friends were captured by the Babylonians. The king of Babylon wanted them to work for him. The king wanted them to eat his rich food and drink his wine. But Daniel said, "No! This would not please our God." So Daniel and his friends ate vegetables and drank water. At the end of ten days they were stronger than anyone who ate the king's food. The king saw this and was pleased. God was pleased, too. God gave Daniel and his friends wisdom to help the king. We should also take good care of our bodies so we can be strong to do what God commands.

Which Way to Good Health?

Should Daniel eat snacks or good food if he wants to be strong for God? Help him find the way to the best food.

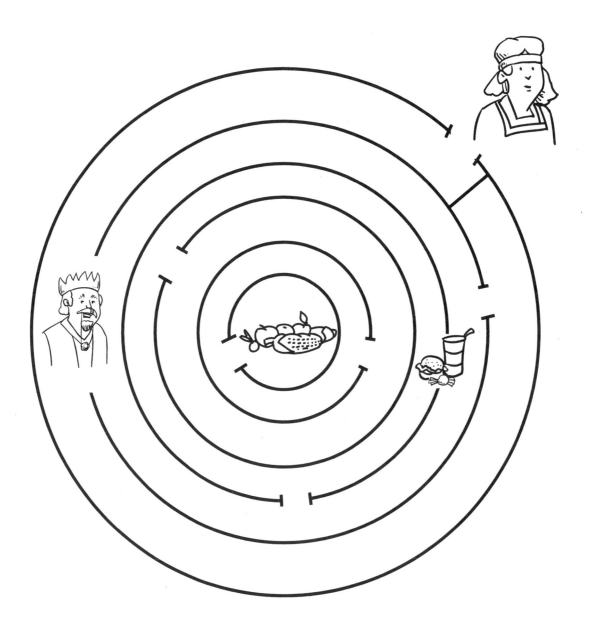

Three Friends Obey God

Memory Verse

We know that an idol is nothing at all.
~1 Corinthians 8:4

Teacher Talk

Say, The king asked Daniel's three friends named Shadrach, Meshach and Abednego to bow down to an idol. They refused and the king became angry. He threw Daniel's friends into a hot, fiery furnace. But God took care of them. He will always take care of us when we honor Him.

▶ A Special Visitor

Who did God sent to protect Daniel's friends? Fold this page in the center and then fold outward on the outer dashed lines to discover the special visitor. Color the picture and show your friends!

Daniel in the Lions' Den

Memory Verse

Three times a day he got down on his knees and prayed.
~Daniel 6:10

Teacher Talk

Say, Each day Daniel prayed to God. Some bad men did not like Daniel. They made a rule. They said that the people could only pray to the king. That didn't keep Daniel from praying to God! Then the bad men caught Daniel praying. They threw him into a den of hungry lions. But God saved Daniel!

A Night of Fright?

Daniel spent the night in the lions' den. Can you tell which lion is different? Color it, then color the rest of the picture.

Disobedience Smells Fishy

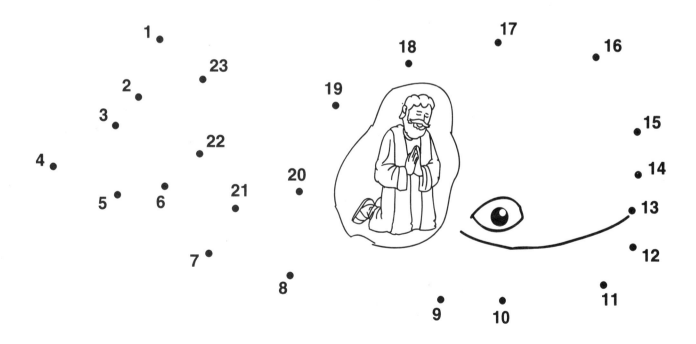

Memory Verse
Jonah ran away from the Lord.
~Jonah 1:3

Teacher Talk
Say, God told Jonah to go to Nineveh. But Jonah hopped on a boat and went the other way. God was not pleased. He sent a storm. The sailors thought Jonah caused the storm so they threw him overboard. God saved Jonah by sending a big fish to swallow him. God doesn't like when we disobey Him, but He will always forgive and save us when we ask.

Swallowed and Saved
Connect the dots to see where Jonah landed when he disobeyed God.

Back on the Road to Nineveh

Memory Verse
Jonah obeyed the word of the Lord and went to Nineveh.
~Jonah 3:3

Teacher Talk
Say, Jonah sat inside the belly of the big fish. He prayed a lot. He thought about how he had disobeyed God. After three days the fish spat Jonah out onto the beach. Jonah had learned his lesson. He obeyed God and headed for Nineveh. Sometimes God has to teach us a lesson when we disobey Him.

Now to Ninevah!
Jonah doesn't want to go the wrong way again. Can you help him find his way to Nineveh?

Teaching Others to Obey

Memory Verse

He will teach us his ways.
~Micah 4:2

Teacher Talk

Say, Jonah told the people of Nineveh that God was not happy with them. The people there worshiped idols instead of God. They listened to Jonah. They changed and worshiped God instead. We should always remember to worship the one, true God.

⋯⋯⋯▶ Where is Jonah?

Nineveh was a crowded city. Jonah told the people to change their ways. Can you find Jonah in the crowd? Color him, then color the rest of the picture.

Jonah

Worshiping God in the Temple

Memory Verse

I...will come into your house; in reverence will I bow down toward your holy temple.
~Psalm 5:7

Teacher Talk

Many people in the Old Testament showed their obedience to God by repairing the temple or worshiping in it. Talk with your children about the importance of caring for God's house. Review some of the stories about people who obeyed God by worshiping in the temple.

·············► A Race to the Temple

Pick a partner, decide which person you will be and see who can get to the temple first.

Doing Everything
God Commands

Memory Verse
I have obeyed the Lord my God; I have done everything you commanded me.
~Deuteronomy 26:14

Teacher Talk
Use this puzzle to review some of the people who obeyed God in the Old Testament. Talk about the ways children can obey everything God commands.

➤ People Who Obeyed God
Can you find the biblical names in the word list by looking up, down and across? Circle the names you find.

Word List
NOAH

MOSES

JOSHUA

DAVID

RUTH

M	N	O	A	H	D
O	Z	X	B	R	A
S	P	Q	O	U	V
E	L	J	O	T	I
S	R	Q	V	H	D
J	O	S	H	U	A

New Testament

Obeying God didn't come any easier just because Jesus was walking the earth. Fortunately, New Testament people had Jesus' example to follow, a life that we strive to emulate today. In the following puzzles and lessons, your students can witness the perfection of Jesus' actions in contrast with those who wrestled with obedience. They will gain a better understanding of how God actually helps us to obey Him and the great rewards that come from doing so.

Mary and Joseph Obey the Angel

Memory Verse
Joseph did what the angel of the Lord had commanded him.
~Matthew 1:24

Teacher Talk
Say, **Several times God sent an angel to tell Joseph what to do for Mary and baby Jesus.** Read to your children the story of Joseph fleeing with Mary and Jesus to Egypt. Discuss how God protects us when we obey Him.

What's Missing?
Finish the second picture in each row.

70

Obeying Your Parents

Memory Verse

[Jesus] was obedient to [his parents].
~Luke 2:51

Teacher Talk

Use the picture to discuss how Jesus helped Joseph and Mary. Say, **Jesus obeyed His parents. God was pleased with Jesus. God is pleased when you obey your parents, too.**

·············► Dad's Helper

Jesus' earthly father, Joseph, was a carpenter. Jesus probably helped him in his work.

Draw a square around the

Draw a line from the ⎡ to the 🪑

Color the 🐱

Run From Satan

Memory Verse
Flee the evil desires of youth.
~2 Timothy 2:22

Teacher Talk
Use the maze to teach the story of Satan tempting Jesus. Say, **Jesus went to the wilderness to pray. Satan knew He was tired and hungry. Jesus ran from Satan and obeyed God.** We should stay away from evil and follow God, too.

Which Way?
Draw a path from Jesus to the open end where He can escape from Satan.

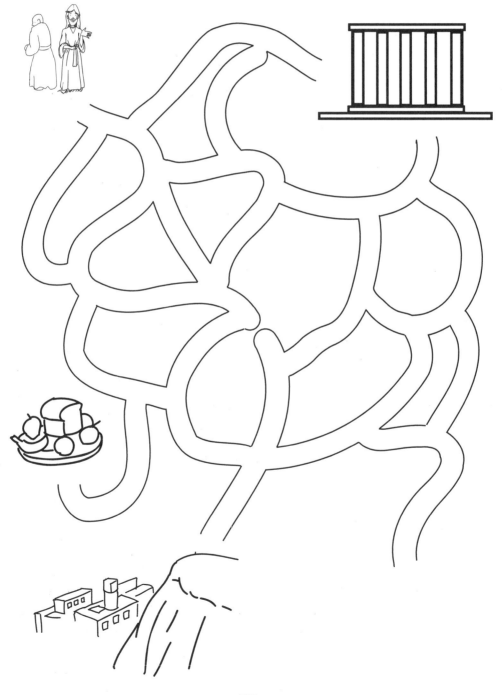

A Story About Some Seeds

Memory Verse
Other seed fell on good soil.
~Luke 8:8

Teacher Talk
Use this activity to tell the story of the parable of the sower. Say, **The ground represents our hearts. The seed is the Bible, God's Word.** Explain to the children what each soil represents. Say, **Each type of ground is like people who obey or disobey the word of God.**

⋯⋯⋯⋯⋯► To Grow or Not to Grow?
In each row, color the picture that is the same as the first picture.

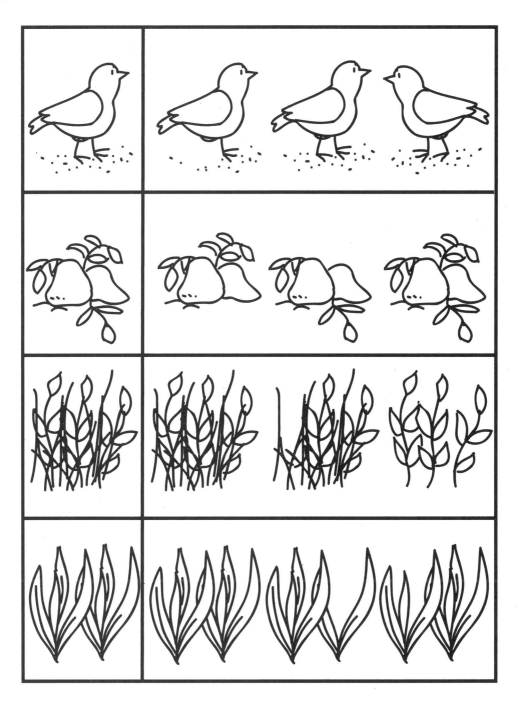

Total Obedience

Memory Verse
Not my will, but yours be done.
~Luke 22:42

Teacher Talk
Say, Jesus showed us what obedience means. He obeyed God and died on a cross for our sin. Jesus did this because He loves us. He wants us to love and obey God.

Jesus Died for Us
Color every space that has a letter from the word OBEY in it to see a gift from God.

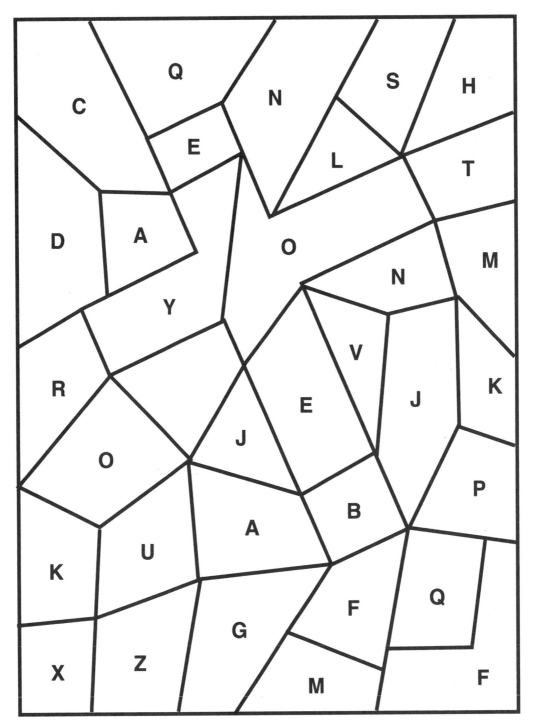

74

The Winds Obey Jesus

Memory Verse
Even the wind and the waves obey him!
~Mark 4:41

Teacher Talk
Use this story to teach your children that Jesus is in control of everything. Say, **Jesus'** disciples found themselves in the middle of a terrible storm. Jesus was asleep in the boat. The disciples were afraid and woke up Jesus. Jesus told the winds and the waves to be still. Immediately all was quiet.

In Control
Draw a ☐ around the ⚡

Draw a line from Jesus to the ◁

Color the ⛵ brown.

Color the 〰 blue.

Twelve Men Follow Jesus

Memory Verse
[Jesus] called his twelve disciples to him.
~Matthew 10:1

Teacher Talk
Say, Many people followed Jesus. However, Jesus called twelve special men to follow and obey Him. They were common men, mostly fishermen. They loved and obeyed Jesus.

How Many Obeyed?
You can find the right number hidden below. Color it one color and the rest of the shapes a different color.

Friends of Jesus

Memory Verse

You are my friends if you do what I command.
~John 15:14

Teacher Talk

Use the Bible story to lead the children in a discussion of how they can love their parents by obeying them. Say, **Jesus talked a lot about obedience to His disciples. He said that love is shared through obedience. What does it show your parents when you obey them?**

⋯⋯⋯⋯▶ Who Obeys Him?

Write the first letter of each object starting with the fish to find the hidden answer in the word circle.

___ ___ ___ ___ ___ ___ ___

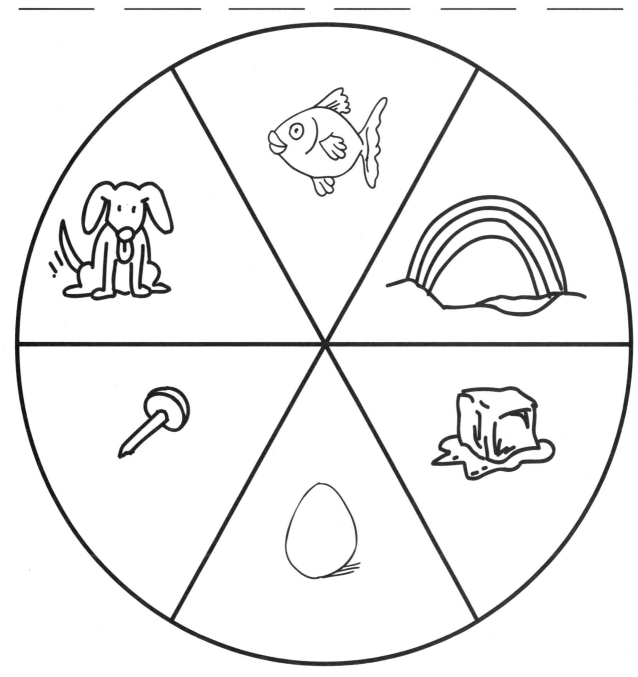

77

Matthew Obeys Jesus

Memory Verse
Matthew got up and followed him.
~Matthew 9:9

Teacher Talk
Say, One day Jesus walked by a man named Matthew sitting in a tax collector's booth. Jesus told Matthew, "Come follow Me." Matthew obeyed Jesus. He left his booth and all his money to follow Jesus.

▸ Matthew Follows Jesus
Can you find 4 things wrong with this picture? Circle them.

Fisherman of Men

Memory Verse

I will make you fishers of men.
~Matthew 4:19

Teacher Talk

Say, Peter was a fisherman. He worked hard. One day Jesus came by. He told Peter, "I will make you a fisherman of men. Leave your net and follow Me." Jesus meant that Peter would teach people to know God. Peter obeyed and followed Jesus. Peter left his net full of fish and followed Jesus. God wants us to follow Him.

·············▶ A Full Catch

Can you count the fish in the net? Color all of the fish. What did Peter learn to catch?

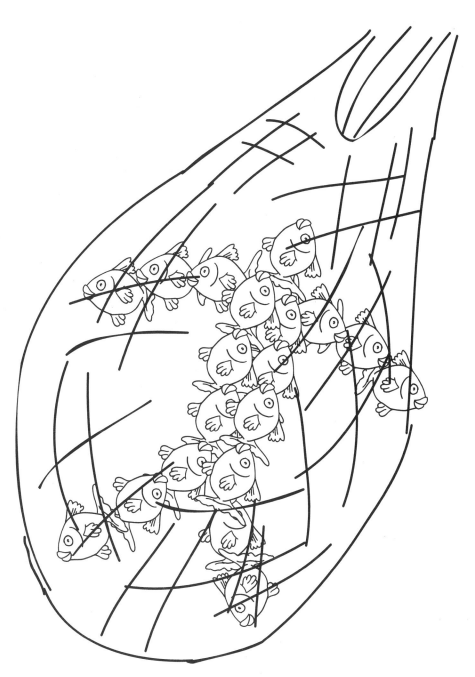

Feed My Sheep

Memory Verse

Whoever has my commands and obeys them, he is the one who loves me.
~John 14:21

Teacher Talk

Say, After He died and came back, Jesus asked Peter several times, "Do you love Me?" Peter answered Jesus, "Yes, Lord, You know that I love You." Jesus was looking beyond Peter's words and reminding him that love for God comes from obedience. One of the greatest commands that Jesus gave was to tell others about Him. By telling Peter to "feed my sheep" Jesus was reminding the disciples to obey Him by taking care of His followers.

Obeying Jesus

There are many ways to feed Jesus' sheep. Draw a line to the pictures that go together.

Zacchaeus Obeys at Once

Memory Verse
Remind the people to be obedient, to be ready to do whatever is good.
~Titus 3:1

Teacher Talk
Use Zacchaeus' example to teach the children about quick obedience. Say, When Jesus saw Zacchaeus in the tree, He told him to come down. Zacchaeus wasted no time obeying Jesus. Do you think Jesus had to count to three to get Zacchaeus to come down from the tree?

⟶ Where Was Zacchaeus?
Connect the dots to find out.

81

Nothing Short of Obedience

Memory Verse

Prove [your] repentance by [your] deeds.
~Acts 26:20

Teacher Talk

Say, Zacchaeus was a tax collector. No one liked him because he collected more money than he should. One day Jesus came to Zacchaeus' town. Because he was too short, Zacchaeus had to climb a tree to see Jesus. Jesus told Zacchaeus to come down from the tree. What do you think Zacchaeus did? We should be just as eager to hear from Jesus as Zacchaeus was!

⋯⋯⋯► Zacchaeus Collected Taxes

These coins are broken and mixed up. Match the two pieces that go together by drawing a line between them.

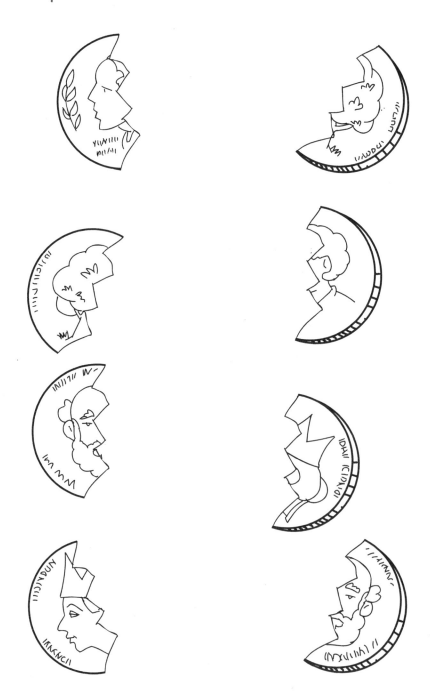

The Holy Spirit Helps Us Obey

Memory Verse

The Holy Spirit will come upon you.
~Luke 1:35

Teacher Talk

Say, Jesus went to heaven. His friends were sad. They prayed and waited for God to show them what to do. One day a fire came down from heaven. A little flame sat on each person's head! This meant that the Holy Spirit had come. The Spirit was from God and it told them what to do. The Spirit helped Jesus' friends obey God. It can help us obey Him, too.

▶ God Sent His Holy Spirit

The flames ABOVE the disciples heads were a sign that God sent His Holy Spirit. Color the flames.

Circle the things that are ABOVE the people. Color the picture.

The People Repent

Memory Verse

Repent and be baptized, every one of you, in the name of Jesus Christ for the forgiveness of your sins.
~Acts 2:38

Teacher Talk

This is a good story to teach children that we should repent as soon as we know we did something wrong. Say, Jerusalem was a crowded city on the day of Pentecost. What a perfect day for the Holy Spirit to show Himself! Peter addressed the crowd and told them the story of Jesus' death and resurrection. Their immediate response was, "Brothers, what shall we do?"

⋯⋯⋯⋯▶ What did Peter Tell the Crowd?

Find the answer by crossing out all of the letters that have a dot in their box.

A	R	E	C	P	E	N	T

A	B	N	C	D	B	F	E

B	D	A	X	P	G	H	T

F	I	J	L	Z	E	M	D

84

Philip Obeys the Angel

Memory Verse

I have promised to obey your words.
~Psalm 119:57

Teacher Talk

Use this story to teach your children that God may have a special plan for each day. Help them understand that they can't always go where they want or do what they want — but God may have someone or something special waiting for them. Say, **God sent an angel to Philip. The angel told Philip to go south. On his journey, Philip met an Ethiopian. Philip taught this man about Jesus. The man decided to follow Jesus, too.**

Go South, Philip

Walk Philip through the maze. Who does he meet?

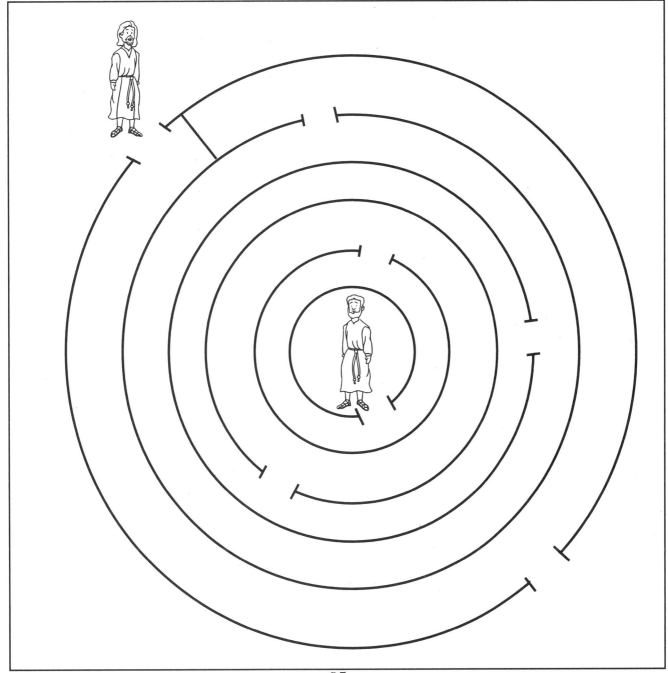

Obeying God's Word

Bible Story:
Acts 8:26-40

Memory Verse

I obey your word.
~Psalm 119:67

Teacher Talk

Use the story puzzle to tell the story of the Ethiopian and Philip. Say, **One day a very important man drove his chariot from Jerusalem. He was on his way home to Ethiopia. God sent Philip to meet the man. Philip saw the man reading a scroll. The scroll was God's Word. Philip helped the man to understand the scroll. The Ethiopian obeyed God and received Jesus as his Savior. God wants us to tell others about Him.**

Mixed-Up Story

These pictures tell the story of the Ethiopian and Philip. But they are in the wrong order! Number them in the order that the story happened. The first one is done for you.

Saul Obeys God

Memory Verse
My heart is changed within me.
~Hosea 11:8

Teacher Talk
Say, Saul hated anyone who followed Jesus. He did not want people to obey Jesus. He even killed some people. One day Jesus said to Saul, "Stop hurting Me." Saul then knew that Jesus was God's Son. He stopped hurting Jesus' friends. From that time on Saul obeyed God. It hurts Jesus when we do not follow Him.

Saul Changes His Ways
Color the picture by following the code.
1=Brown
2=Green
3=Yellow
4=Blue
5=Red
6=Black
7=Orange

Starting New Churches

Memory Verse
I love the house where you live.
~Psalm 26:8

Teacher Talk
Explain that Saul changed his name to Paul. Say, Now that he obeyed God, many people hated Paul. But he made new friends who loved Jesus. Paul and his new friends traveled to far away places. They told people about Jesus. They started new churches everywhere they went. Jesus is happy when we tell others about Him. Help the younger children learn to play the game and add up their scores.

Paul's Missionary Trips: A Game for Two People
Players should choose a ship or a man and follows its line until they come to a church. Then they should color the church and tally the number. When all of the churches have been colored, the player with the highest score wins.

Praises in Prison

Memory Verse

I will praise the Lord.
~Psalm 146:2

Teacher Talk

Say, Paul continued to tell people about Jesus. Many people hated Paul. One day some bad men put Paul and his friend Silas in jail. But Paul and Silas trusted God. They never stopped obeying Him. While in prison Paul and Silas sang about Jesus. God loves to hear our songs of praise.

⋯⋯⋯➤ Paul and Silas

There are 5 things wrong in this picture. Can you find them? Circle them, then color the picture.

Dorcas Loves Jesus

Memory Verse
Love each other as I have loved you.
~John 15:12

Teacher Talk
Say, Dorcas was always helping others. She listened when they were sad. She fed them when they had no food. She helped them when they were sick. Dorcas' favorite thing to do was to make clothes for people. Dorcas knew that to love and obey Jesus, she must love others and take care of them.

Go-Togethers
In each row, color the pictures that belong together.

Stay at Our House

Memory Verse

They shared everything they had.
~Acts 4:32

Teacher Talk

Say, Paul made friends wherever he traveled. He had two special friends, a woman named Priscilla and her husband, Aquila. Priscilla and Aquila made tents and Paul helped them. Paul preached at a church that met in their home. Priscilla and Aquila obeyed God by letting Paul stay at their house. We can show God's love by sharing what we have, too.

Making Tents

There are four tents in this picture. Color the ones that are exactly alike the same color.

Cloud of Witnesses

Memory Verse
If you love me, you will obey.
~John 14:15

Teacher Talk
Use this game to review lessons from this book. Say, **The Bible tells us about many people who obeyed God. We can learn how to obey God by remembering their stories. Here is a game to help us remember people who obeyed God.** Help younger children learn to play the game.

Obedience Game
Each player gets a game board. Take turns tossing a coin to move. "Tails" moves one space and "Heads" moves two spaces. If you land on a picture of a person you must tell how that person obeyed God. If you answer correctly, then use the jump-ahead path. The first player to reach the cloud of witnesses on his or her game wins.

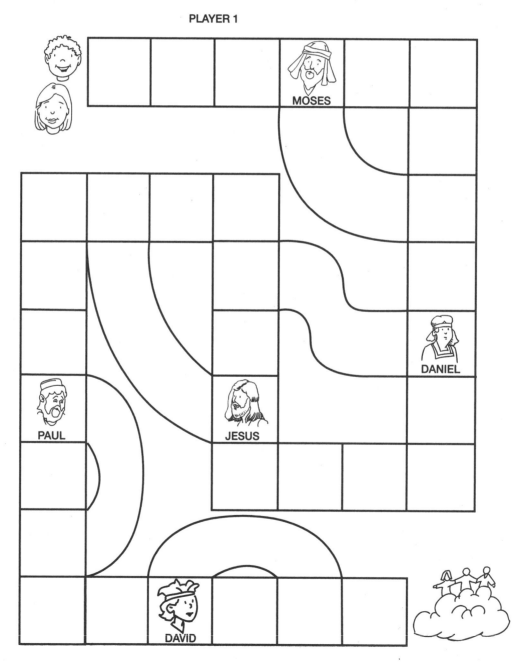

PLAYER 1

92

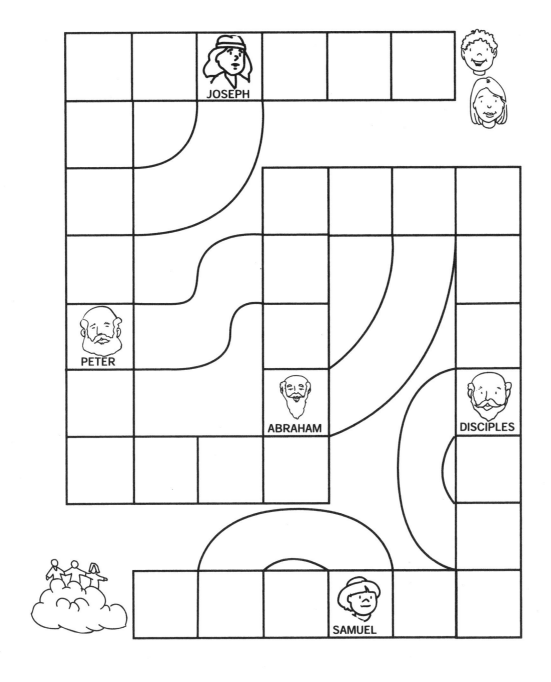

Whom Do I Obey?

Memory Verse

Obey your leaders.
Hebrews 13:17

Teacher Talk

Say, Young children understand the importance of obeying their parents, but may not know that there are others they should obey as well. Use this activity to discuss the different people in our lives that God uses to help us. Talk about how we can obey these people. Say, **God is happy when we obey these special helpers.**

▶ Match the Pictures

Draw a line from the children to the special helper they are obeying.

Answers

p. 10, row 1: second ark; row 2: first pair of turtles; row 3: first bird; row 4: first pair of butterflies; row 5: second cloud

p. 12

p. 14, CANAAN

p. 15, nine

p. 16, baby

p. 18, row 1: third sheep missing ear; row 2: second basket missing handle; row 3: fourth sheave missing top; row 4: third jar missing handles

p. 20, clockwise from top left: 1,4,2,3

p. 23, three frogs; six locusts; eight flies

p. 24

p. 25, dots form the Ten Commandment tablets

p. 26, "Obey Your Mother and Father" matches boy helping man; "Make God's Day Special" matches people going to church; "Do Not Steal" matches child taking candy.

p. 27, HEART

p. 28, disobedient children are in right column

p. 30, dots form a flame

p. 31, jars are 1 second row, 1 third row, 1 fourth row; swords are 1 first row, 2 second row, 1 third row, 2 fourth row; torches are 3 first row, 3 second row, 1 third row, 3 fourth row

p. 32, squares = five
circles = six
triangles = eight

p. 34, row 1: different one is last; row 2: different one is second; row 3: different one is third; row 4: different one is second

p. 35, In bottom picture: Ruth has no vest, a tied belt and no shoes; Naomi has no hair bangs, no ear, no head band, no belt and no shoes.

p. 36, sheaves of grain

p. 37

p. 38, top left column and second right column; second left column and bottom right column; third left column and third right column; bottom left column and top right column

p. 39, lamb is at head of bed; oil lamp is in pillow; water pitcher is near foot of bed; scroll is in fold of sheet; patched robe is at foot of bed

p. 40, eleven

p. 42, In bottom picture: soldier behind David; David wearing helmet; David carrying bow, arrows and sword; Goliath missing helmet; Goliath missing sword; Goliath wearing tied vest

p. 43, THEY DO WHAT A FRIEND ASKS

p. 44, All of the seated children should be colored.

p. 45

p. 46, top picture: idol; bottom picture: friends

p. 48, The black and yellow colors reveal a raven.

p. 49, In bottom picture: Elijah is not pointing and has no mustache; Elisha has no headband; three stones are missing from the path; a cloud is missing from behind Elijah's head; a stone is missing from the field

p. 50, HE THREW SALT ON THE WATER

p. 51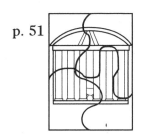

p. 53, PRIDE

p. 54, the top left stone fits the bottom right space; the bottom left stone fits the top right space; the top right stone fits the bottom left space; and the bottom right stone fits the top left space

p. 55, The horse is in the right side of the wall, facing the left.

p. 56, Lines should be drawn from Esther to the long dress, fancy shoes, necklace and crown.

p. 57, Esther is at top left

p. 58, clockwise from top left: 1,3,2,4

p. 59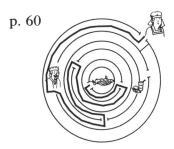

p. 60

p. 61, Folded picture will show an angel.

p. 62, Lion at bottom has upward tail.

p. 63, dots form a whale

p. 64

p. 65, Jonah is in the center

p. 66

p. 67

p. 70, row 1: second angel missing feet; row 2: second man missing bag on roll and camel missing one back leg; row 3: manger missing back left slat; row 4: second picture missing sun

p. 72

p. 73, row 1: second bird; row 2: third plant; row 3: first plant; row 4: first leaves

p. 74, Colored puzzle reveals a cross.

p. 76, Colored puzzle reveals the number 12.

p. 77, FRIEND

p. 78, tree is upside-down; car on street; man is wearing polka dots; bull is eating money

p. 79, Men

p. 80, top left goes with bottom right; middle left goes with top right; bottom left goes with middle right

p. 81, Dots form a tree

p. 82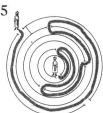

p. 84, REPENT AND BE BAPTIZED

p. 85

p. 86, Clockwise from top right: 1,4,2,3

p. 89, What is wrong: balloons; mouse with cat tail; mittens on right man; right man's stool missing leg; left man missing shoe

p. 90, cloth, tape, thread; shoes, jacket, robe; bread, meat, apple; glass, bowl, plate

p. 91, The two right tents are the same.

p. 94, top left matches bottom right; second on left matches third on right; third on left matches top on right; bottom on left matches second on right